SUPERCONDUCTIVITY AND AI

SYNTHESIS OF POTENTIAL TO NEW FRONTIERS

KING SMARTY

Table Of Content

Introduction

In "Synthesis of Potential," we embark on an intellectual journey, uncovering the remarkable intersection between two groundbreaking scientific fields: Artificial Intelligence (AI) and Superconductivity. This book serves as a captivating exploration into the powerful symbiosis of these disciplines, demonstrating how they have revolutionized our understanding of nature, opened new realms of possibilities, and ignited a paradigm shift in science and technology.

Introduction of Superconductivity

Superconductivity is a fascinating phenomenon in physics where certain materials exhibit zero electrical resistance and expel magnetic fields when cooled below a critical temperature. This critical temperature is specific to each superconducting material and typically lies well below room temperature.

When a material becomes superconducting, it allows electric current to flow through it without any loss of energy due to resistance. This means that once a current is set up in a superconducting loop, it can persist indefinitely without any external power source, creating a persistent current loop. This property has significant implications for energy efficiency and various applications in electrical engineering.

Superconductors can also expel magnetic fields, a phenomenon known as the Meissner effect. This means that when a superconductor is exposed to an external magnetic field, it generates a current that cancels out the magnetic field inside the material, causing the magnetic flux to be expelled from the material. This property makes superconductors useful in applications such as levitating trains (Maglev trains) and other magnetic levitation devices.

Superconductivity was first discovered in 1911 by Dutch physicist Heike Kamerlingh Onnes when he observed mercury's behavior at very low temperatures. However, it was only in the latter half of the 20th century that significant progress was made in understanding and engineering superconductors for practical applications.

Superconductors have found use in various fields, including power transmission, magnetic resonance imaging (MRI) machines, particle accelerators, sensitive scientific instruments, and quantum computing research. While superconductors hold great promise, one of the major challenges is achieving and maintaining the extremely low temperatures required for their superconducting state, which limits their widespread adoption in some applications. Nonetheless, ongoing research continues to push the boundaries of superconductivity and explore new materials with higher critical temperatures and improved properties.

Chapter 1

The Genesis of AI

Journey through the fascinating history of Artificial Intelligence, exploring its humble beginnings and the transformative breakthroughs that have led to the AI revolution we witness today.

1.1 The Roots of AI:

We start by delving into the early ideas and concepts that laid the foundation for AI. From ancient myths and tales of artificial beings to the philosophical ponderings of ancient civilizations, we uncover the roots of humanity's fascination with creating intelligent machines.

1.2 The Birth of Computing:

As we move forward in time, we explore the birth of modern computing and how it provided the essential tools for the realization of AI. The contributions of pioneers like Alan Turing and Ada Lovelace are highlighted, along with the development of early programmable machines.

1.3 The Dartmouth Conference and the Birth of AI:

One of the key moments in AI's history was the Dartmouth Conference in 1956, where the term "Artificial Intelligence" was coined. We delve into the ambitious goals set by AI pioneers at the conference and how it marked the formal beginning of AI as a scientific discipline.

1.4 The AI Winter:

AI's journey was not always smooth sailing. We explore the periods known as the "AI winter," where early optimism was met with significant challenges and setbacks, leading to reduced funding and interest in AI research. Despite the setbacks, dedicated researchers continued to push the boundaries of AI.

1.5 The Rise of Expert Systems:

In the 1980s, expert systems emerged as a prominent AI application, showcasing the potential of AI to solve specific problems with human-like expertise. We examine the impact of expert systems in various industries and how they laid the groundwork for more sophisticated AI techniques.

1.6 Machine Learning and Neural Networks:

This section focuses on the resurgence of AI in the late 20th century, driven by the advent of machine learning techniques and neural networks. We explore the development of algorithms that allowed computers to learn from data and make predictions without explicit programming.

1.7 The AI Revolution:

The pivotal moment when machine learning surpassed human capabilities in specific tasks is a highlight of this section. We discuss milestones such as Deep Blue defeating the world chess champion and AlphaGo's victory against human Go players, which marked significant turning points in AI history.

1.8 Deep Learning and Big Data:

Deep learning, a subset of machine learning, gained prominence for its ability to handle complex problems by leveraging vast amounts of data. We delve into the role of big data and the explosion of computing power in driving the success of deep learning algorithms.

1.9 AI in Everyday Life:

As we conclude the chapter, we showcase the pervasive presence of AI in our daily lives, from virtual assistants and recommendation systems to image recognition and language translation. We reflect on how AI has become an integral part of the modern world and discuss the ethical considerations that come with its widespread adoption.

Chapter 1 sets the stage for the book's exploration of the synergy between AI and superconductivity. It serves as a foundation for understanding the transformative power of AI and how it has propelled us into an era of boundless possibilities and scientific discovery.

Chapter 2

AI in Scientific Inquiry

In this chapter, "AI in Scientific Inquiry," we embark on a thrilling expedition to explore how Artificial Intelligence has become an indispensable tool in scientific research, uncovering the hidden secrets of the universe and accelerating progress across various disciplines.

2.1 AI and the Cosmos:

We begin with a cosmic journey, showcasing how AI is revolutionizing our understanding of the universe. From processing data collected by space telescopes to detecting distant exoplanets and studying cosmic phenomena, AI algorithms have allowed astronomers to delve deeper into the cosmos than ever before.

2.2 Unraveling the Genetic Code:

In this section, we dive into the realm of biology and genetics. AI's ability to analyze vast genomic datasets has led to groundbreaking discoveries in understanding the human genome and identifying genetic variations associated with diseases. We explore how AI is transforming personalized medicine and opening new avenues for targeted treatments.

2.3 Climate Modeling and Environmental Impact:

Climate change and environmental challenges are urgent global issues. We investigate how AI-driven climate models are enhancing our predictions of weather patterns, ocean currents, and climate trends. AI's power to process enormous amounts of environmental data is helping scientists formulate informed policies for sustainability and conservation efforts.

2.4 High-Energy Physics and Particle Accelerators:

Venturing into the world of particle physics, we explore how AI plays a vital role in analyzing the massive amounts of data generated by particle accelerators like the Large Hadron Collider (LHC). Discover how AI is accelerating discoveries, enabling the detection of elusive particles, and probing the fundamental building blocks of matter.

2.5 Drug Discovery and Healthcare Advancements:

AI's prowess in drug discovery and medical research is undeniable. We delve into the revolutionary impact of AI in identifying potential drug candidates, streamlining clinical trials, and enhancing medical image analysis. The fusion of AI and superconductivity in healthcare applications is discussed, opening new possibilities for magnetic resonance imaging (MRI) and other diagnostic techniques.

2.6 Environmental Monitoring and Biodiversity Conservation:

AI's role in monitoring and conserving the environment is explored, showcasing how AI-driven systems are employed in tracking endangered species, detecting deforestation, and assessing the health of ecosystems. We discuss the potential of superconducting sensors in enhancing environmental monitoring capabilities.

2.7 AI and Materials Science:

Materials science has seen remarkable advancements with the aid of AI. Discover how machine learning algorithms are revolutionizing the search for new materials with specific properties, such as superconductors with higher critical temperatures and improved performance.

2.8 The Power of Data Fusion:

In this section, we highlight the transformative potential of combining data from multiple scientific disciplines. The fusion of AI with superconductivity allows for enhanced data analysis and simulations, opening new avenues for interdisciplinary research.

Conclusion:

Chapter 2 concludes with a reflection on how AI has become an indispensable tool in scientific inquiry. From the grand scales of the universe to the intricacies of the human genome, AI's data processing prowess has accelerated scientific discovery, providing profound insights into the fundamental laws that govern our world. The synergy between AI and superconductivity holds the promise of even greater breakthroughs, unveiling new frontiers of knowledge and inspiring future generations to continue their quest for understanding and innovation.

Chapter 3

The Superconductivity Odyssey

Welcome to the enigmatic world of superconductivity! In this chapter, we embark on a captivating journey through the history, discoveries, challenges, and potential of superconductivity. From its serendipitous discovery to its revolutionary applications, we explore the awe-inspiring properties of superconductors and their impact on various scientific and technological fields.

3.1 *A Serendipitous Discovery:*

Our odyssey begins with the accidental discovery of superconductivity in 1911 by Dutch physicist Heike Kamerlingh Onnes. We delve into the groundbreaking moment when he observed mercury's electrical resistance vanishing at extremely low temperatures, opening the door to a new era of physics.

3.2 *The Quest for High-Temperature Superconductors:*

We examine the historical milestones in the pursuit of high-temperature superconductors. Discover the excitement that ensued when researchers achieved superconductivity at temperatures closer to liquid nitrogen levels, marking a turning point in practical applications.

3.3 *Understanding Superconductivity:*

Delving deeper into the science, we explore the quantum mechanical principles behind superconductivity. Readers will gain insights into Cooper pairs, the Meissner effect, and the energy gap phenomenon that underpins the behavior of superconducting materials.

3.4 *The Different Classes of Superconductors*:

Superconductors come in various classes, each with distinct properties and potential applications. We explore Type I and Type II superconductors, as well as unconventional superconductors like high-temperature cuprates and iron-based superconductors. Each class holds unique promise and challenges in harnessing their capabilities.

3.5 *Superconductivity and Quantum Computing*:

The marriage of superconductivity and quantum computing is a major highlight of this section. We delve into the concept of superconducting qubits and their role in quantum information processing. Learn how these quantum bits have paved the way for quantum supremacy and the race for quantum advantage.

3.6 *Superconductors in Electromagnetic Applications*:

Superconductors have revolutionized electromagnetic technologies. From powerful magnets used in medical MRI machines to high-field magnets in particle accelerators, we uncover how superconductors have dramatically enhanced the capabilities of these applications.

3.7 *Superconductivity for Sustainable Energy*:

In this section, we discuss the potential role of superconductivity in sustainable energy solutions. From the development of superconducting power cables that reduce energy losses during transmission to superconducting generators for wind turbines, we explore how superconductors contribute to a greener energy future.

3.8 *Challenges and Future Prospects:*

While superconductors hold immense promise, several challenges stand in the way of their widespread adoption. We examine the technological hurdles and materials limitations that researchers are working to overcome. Additionally, we explore the potential of superconductors in emerging fields like quantum communication and energy storage.

Conclusion:

As our Superconductivity Odyssey comes to a close, we reflect on the remarkable journey we've undertaken. From its accidental discovery to its diverse applications, superconductivity has transformed science and technology, opening doors to quantum computing, renewable energy, and beyond.

The synergy between AI and superconductivity promises to revolutionize both fields, propelling us toward a future where the boundaries of human knowledge and capability are continually pushed to new frontiers. Together, AI and superconductivity hold the potential to create sustainable energy solutions, enhance scientific discovery, and unlock the mysteries of the universe, inspiring us to pursue knowledge and innovation with renewed vigor and determination.

Chapter 4

AI Meets Superconductivity

Introduction:

The extraordinary synergy between Artificial Intelligence (AI) and superconductivity, unveiling the transformative impact of their collaboration. Explore how AI-driven simulations and machine learning algorithms have revolutionized the search for novel superconducting materials, optimized critical temperature predictions, and designed custom-tailored compounds, ushering in a new era of superconductivity research.

4.1 The Quest for High-Temperature Superconductors:

We begin by highlighting the historical efforts to discover high-temperature superconductors. The challenges in achieving practical superconductivity at higher temperatures and the importance of finding materials with elevated critical temperatures are discussed.

4.2 Accelerating Material Discovery with AI:

AI has become an indispensable tool in the discovery of novel materials, and its application to superconductivity research has proven revolutionary. We explore how machine learning algorithms efficiently navigate vast databases of materials properties, accelerating the identification of potential superconductors with previously unforeseen properties.

4.3 Predictive Modeling and Simulation:

AI-driven simulations have become a game-changer in understanding superconducting materials at the atomic level. We delve into the techniques used to model the behavior of materials, predict critical temperatures, and gain insights into the underlying mechanisms of superconductivity.

4.4 *Optimizing Critical Temperature Predictions*:

AI's data processing capabilities have enabled researchers to optimize critical temperature predictions for specific superconducting materials. We showcase examples where machine learning algorithms have refined predictions, leading to the discovery of previously elusive high-temperature superconductors.

4.5 *Designing Custom-Tailored Superconductors:*

The marriage of AI and superconductivity has unlocked the potential to design custom-tailored superconducting compounds. By leveraging machine learning algorithms, scientists can fine-tune material properties to meet specific requirements for various applications, from power transmission to quantum computing.

4.6 *Materials by Design*:

The concept of "materials by design" becomes a reality with the integration of AI into superconductivity research. We explore how AI-driven approaches have transformed the trial-and-error approach to materials discovery, making it possible to predict and synthesize superconducting materials with targeted properties.

4.7 *Advancing Superconducting Applications:*

AI's impact on superconductivity extends beyond materials discovery. We showcase how machine learning algorithms are optimizing the performance of superconducting devices, such as MRI systems, particle accelerators, and energy-efficient power transmission technologies.

4.8 Quantum Simulations and AI:

AI also plays a significant role in the burgeoning field of quantum simulations. We discuss how AI-driven simulations aid in understanding complex quantum phenomena relevant to superconductivity, paving the way for advancements in quantum computing and quantum materials research.

Conclusion:

Chapter 4 concludes with a celebration of the powerful union between AI and superconductivity. The integration of AI-driven simulations, machine learning algorithms, and data processing capabilities has revolutionized the search for novel superconducting materials, optimized critical temperature predictions, and unlocked the potential for designing custom-tailored compounds. This chapter provides a glimpse of the immense possibilities that lie ahead, as AI continues to propel superconductivity research towards new frontiers, ushering in a future where superconductors find applications in areas previously considered science fiction. The collaboration between AI and superconductivity stands as a testament to the potential of interdisciplinary research and the limitless possibilities that arise when diverse fields converge in the quest for knowledge and innovation.

Chapter 5

Supercharging Energy Efficiency

In this chapter, "Supercharging Energy Efficiency," we embark on a journey to discover how superconductivity has transformed the landscape of power transmission and distribution, leading to a greener and more sustainable energy future. Explore the revolutionary development of superconducting cables, the game-changing potential of energy storage technologies, and the crucial role of AI-optimized superconductors in reshaping the global energy landscape.

5.1 *The Challenge of Energy Transmission*:

We begin by examining the challenges in traditional energy transmission and distribution systems. Losses due to resistance in conventional power lines contribute to energy wastage, inefficiency, and environmental impacts. We set the stage for how superconductivity can be a game-changer in addressing these issues.

5.2 *Superconducting Cables: The Path to Efficiency:*

Introducing superconducting cables, we explore how these remarkable materials can carry electricity with zero resistance, eliminating energy losses during transmission. We discuss the technological advancements that have made long-distance superconducting power transmission a reality, promising a significant reduction in energy wastage.

5.3 *High-Capacity Power Grids:*

Superconducting cables pave the way for high-capacity power grids that can efficiently deliver electricity over long distances. We delve into the potential of these grids to facilitate the integration of renewable energy sources into existing power systems, enabling a more robust and flexible energy infrastructure.

5.4 *Energy Storage Revolution*:

AI-optimized superconductors play a pivotal role in revolutionizing energy storage technologies. We explore the development of superconducting energy storage systems, which have the potential to store vast amounts of energy and release it on demand, helping stabilize power grids and accommodate intermittent renewable energy sources.

5.5 *Magnetic Energy Storage*:

Magnetic energy storage systems utilizing superconductors offer a breakthrough in energy storage density and efficiency. We discuss the working principles of these systems and how AI-driven simulations enhance their performance, making them a promising candidate for large-scale energy storage applications.

5.6 *Superconductivity in Renewable Energy*:

We explore the symbiotic relationship between superconductivity and renewable energy sources. From enhancing the efficiency of wind turbines to improving the performance of solar energy systems, AI-optimized superconductors enable a seamless integration of renewable energy into the global energy mix.

5.7 *The Promise of Superconducting Generators*:

Superconducting generators have the potential to revolutionize energy production. We discuss how these generators, coupled with AI-driven optimization techniques, can significantly increase energy efficiency and reduce greenhouse gas emissions.

5.8 *Grid Modernization and Smart Grids*:

AI and superconductivity are driving the modernization of power grids into smart grids. We showcase how AI algorithms optimize energy flow, detect faults, and enhance grid stability, making energy distribution more efficient, reliable, and resilient.

Conclusion:

Chapter 5 concludes with a vision of a brighter and greener energy future, enabled by the marriage of superconductivity and AI. The development of superconducting cables, revolutionary energy storage technologies, and AI-optimized superconductors have paved the way for a more efficient, sustainable, and resilient energy landscape. As these innovations continue to evolve, they offer hope for a world where energy is harnessed and utilized with minimal waste and environmental impact. Superconductivity's potential to supercharge energy efficiency stands as a testament to the power of interdisciplinary research and innovation in creating a sustainable future for generations to come.

Chapter 6

Beyond Levitation - Superconductors in Transport

In this chapter, "Beyond Levitation - Superconductors in Transport," we embark on an exciting journey into the world of transportation and witness the marvels of magnetic levitation and cutting-edge Maglev systems powered by superconductivity. From supersonic trains that glide effortlessly to spacecraft propulsion systems, we explore how AI-driven design has revolutionized transportation, paving the way for efficient, eco-friendly, and futuristic mobility solutions.

6.1 *Magnetic Levitation: The Principle Unveiled:*

We begin by unraveling the principles of magnetic levitation and how superconductivity plays a pivotal role in this revolutionary transportation concept. Understanding the basics of electromagnetic forces allows us to comprehend how magnetic levitation eliminates friction and enables high-speed, contactless transportation.

6.2 *Maglev Trains: Defying Gravity with Speed*:

Introducing Maglev trains, we explore how these advanced transportation systems leverage superconductors and powerful electromagnets to achieve ultra-high speeds. We showcase Maglev projects worldwide, witnessing how AI-driven design has optimized their performance, efficiency, and safety.

6.3 *Supersonic Trains: Blazing New Trails*:

The fusion of superconductivity and AI extends beyond Maglev to supersonic trains. We delve into the development of supersonic transportation and how AI optimization enhances their aerodynamics and energy efficiency, revolutionizing long-distance travel.

6.4 *Magnetic Launch Systems: Propelling Spacecraft to New Heights:*

AI-driven design has also found its way into space transportation. We explore how superconducting magnetic launch systems can propel spacecraft into orbit more efficiently, reducing the need for traditional rocket propellants and minimizing environmental impact.

6.5 *Urban Mobility: The Promise of Maglev Pods:*

AI-driven, superconducting Maglev pods promise to revolutionize urban mobility. We discuss how these autonomous and eco-friendly transportation solutions are reshaping city landscapes and offering efficient alternatives to traditional commuting methods.

6.6 *Hyperloop: The Future of High-Speed Travel:*

The chapter further delves into Hyperloop, an ambitious transportation concept that combines Maglev technology with low-pressure tubes for even higher speeds. We explore how AI and superconductivity drive the development of this transformative mode of transportation.

6.7 *Superconducting Electric Vehicles:*

Superconductivity's impact on transportation extends to electric vehicles (EVs). We examine how superconducting materials are enhancing EV battery efficiency, leading to longer ranges and faster charging times.

6.8 *AI-Optimized Transport Networks:*

AI's role in optimizing transport networks is explored, showcasing how machine learning algorithms enhance traffic management, reduce congestion, and improve overall transportation efficiency.

Conclusion:

Chapter 6 concludes with a visionary outlook on the future of transportation, where superconductors and AI continue to power cutting-edge transportation solutions. From Maglev trains defying gravity to supersonic travel and space propulsion systems, the fusion of superconductivity and AI is shaping a new era of efficient, eco-friendly, and futuristic mobility. As these technologies evolve, they promise to revolutionize how we move and connect, bringing us closer to a more sustainable and interconnected world. The convergence of superconductivity and AI in transportation stands as a testament to human ingenuity and our collective efforts to reshape the way we travel, opening new horizons for the mobility of tomorrow.

Chapter 7

Quantum Horizons

Introduction:

We embark on an exciting journey into the fascinating world of quantum computing, where the convergence of superconductivity and AI unlocks unprecedented computational power and potential. We explore how superconducting quantum devices enable quantum computing breakthroughs, understand the implications of quantum computing's immense processing power, and witness how AI algorithms play a crucial role in overcoming inherent quantum limitations.

7.1 The Quantum Revolution:

We begin by providing a brief overview of the quantum revolution, highlighting the fundamental principles of quantum mechanics that underpin quantum computing. The unique properties of superconductors that make them ideal candidates for building quantum devices are also introduced.

7.2 *Superconducting Quantum Bits (Qubits):*

Explore how superconducting qubits serve as the building blocks of quantum computing. We delve into the principles of superposition and entanglement that enable quantum information processing, paving the way for a new era of computing power.

7.3 *Quantum Computing Power:*

Understand the implications of quantum computing's immense processing power. We showcase how quantum algorithms can exponentially outperform classical algorithms for specific tasks, heralding breakthroughs in cryptography, optimization, and simulating complex systems.

7.4 *Quantum Error Correction*:

Inherent quantum limitations such as decoherence and errors pose significant challenges to quantum computing. We explore how AI-driven error correction algorithms offer solutions to enhance the stability and reliability of quantum computations.

7.5 *Quantum Machine Learning*:

Witness the symbiotic relationship between quantum computing and AI, as quantum machine learning emerges as a powerful field. We explore how AI algorithms and quantum computing can mutually enhance each other, promising revolutionary advancements in data analysis and pattern recognition.

7.6 *Quantum Simulation and Materials Discovery*:

AI-driven quantum simulation holds the potential to revolutionize materials discovery. We examine how quantum computers, powered by superconducting qubits, can efficiently simulate the behavior of complex materials, leading to the discovery of new superconductors and other advanced materials.

7.7 *Quantum Cryptography and AI Security:*

AI's role in enhancing quantum cryptography and quantum-safe algorithms is discussed. We explore how quantum computing's ability to break classical encryption algorithms necessitates the development of AI-driven quantum-resistant cryptographic methods.

7.8 *The Path to Quantum Advantage:*

The quest for quantum advantage—the point where quantum computers surpass classical supercomputers—becomes a focal point. We discuss the challenges, milestones, and potential applications that will bring us closer to achieving quantum advantage.

Conclusion:

Chapter 7 concludes with a glimpse into the quantum horizons where superconductivity and AI intersect to unlock the full potential of quantum computing. The integration of superconducting qubits, quantum algorithms, and AI-driven error correction promises to revolutionize computation, leading to groundbreaking advancements in science, technology, and security. The quantum revolution, fueled by the synergy of superconductivity and AI, offers a glimpse of a future where seemingly impossible tasks become achievable and quantum computing becomes an integral part of our daily lives. As researchers and engineers continue to explore the quantum realm, we are poised on the cusp of transformative breakthroughs that will shape the course of computing and scientific inquiry for generations to come.

Conclusion

The Fusion of Synergy

In this final chapter, we stand in awe of the remarkable fusion of AI and superconductivity, a union that has surpassed expectations and illuminated a path towards addressing some of the most pressing global challenges. The convergence of these two groundbreaking fields has opened doors to new frontiers, pushing the boundaries of what was once considered impossible, and transforming the landscape of science, technology, and innovation.

The Power of Sustainable Energy:

The marriage of AI and superconductivity has revolutionized the realm of sustainable energy. With AI-driven simulations and optimization techniques, we have witnessed the development of high-temperature superconductors, superconducting cables, and energy storage solutions that promise efficient power transmission, reduced energy wastage, and cleaner electricity generation. Our journey has unveiled a greener and more sustainable energy landscape, one that offers hope for a future where renewable sources power our world.

Medical Marvels and Scientific Inquiry:

AI's data processing prowess has transformed scientific research across various domains. In conjunction with superconductivity, AI-driven simulations have accelerated the discovery of novel materials, aided drug development, and propelled advancements in genetic research. The integration of AI and superconductivity has catalyzed breakthroughs in medical imaging, quantum computing, and materials science, paving the way for medical marvels and scientific discoveries that were once beyond our imagination.

Transportation Beyond Imagination:

The extraordinary alliance of AI and superconductivity has redefined transportation. Magnetic levitation and Maglev systems have revolutionized travel, enabling efficient, high-speed, and eco-friendly transportation options like never before. The future of urban mobility, supersonic trains, and even space propulsion systems hold promise for a transformative transportation landscape that reshapes the way we connect and explore.

Quantum Horizons Unveiled:

Our exploration into the quantum realm has showcased the immense power of quantum computing, facilitated by superconducting qubits and augmented by AI-driven optimization and error correction techniques. The potential for quantum advantage and applications in cryptography, quantum simulations, and materials discovery herald a future where quantum computing becomes an indispensable tool for scientific inquiry and technological advancement.

The Infinite Possibilities:

As we conclude this journey, we are left with an overwhelming sense of optimism and wonder. The fusion of AI and superconductivity represents a profound realization of human ingenuity and collaboration. The limitless possibilities that lie ahead, from sustainable energy solutions to quantum computing breakthroughs, have the potential to shape a better future for humanity.

Challenges and Ethical Considerations:

While we celebrate the achievements of AI and superconductivity, we must also acknowledge the challenges and ethical considerations that come with their boundless potential. Ensuring responsible AI use, safeguarding data privacy, and addressing the environmental impacts of superconducting materials production are essential to harnessing the full potential of these technologies for the greater good.

Conclusion

In the fusion of synergy between AI and superconductivity, we find inspiration and hope for a brighter and more sustainable world. The collaborative efforts of scientists, engineers, and innovators have led us on an extraordinary journey of discovery, pushing the boundaries of human knowledge and ingenuity. As we continue to explore the potential of this dynamic partnership, let us approach these transformative technologies with a sense of responsibility and a vision for a future that harnesses their power for the benefit of all humankind. The fusion of AI and superconductivity is not just a scientific pursuit; it is a beacon of hope, guiding us towards solutions that seemed unimaginable just a few decades ago. Together, we embark on a path that leads to new heights of progress, understanding, and innovation.

Bonus Chapter

Advancing Innovation and Creativity in the Fusion of AI and Superconductivity

As "Synthesis of Potential" concludes, we are left with a vision of a world where the fusion of AI and superconductivity propels us towards a brighter, more sustainable future. In this bonus chapter, we offer advice to the scientists, engineers, and visionaries in the field, inspiring them to break more ground and unlock the true potential of this dynamic partnership. By embracing innovation and collaboration, we can harness the power of AI and superconductivity to shape a world where the unimaginable becomes reality.

1.   *Foster   Multidisciplinary Collaboration*:

The fusion of AI and superconductivity inherently requires expertise from multiple disciplines. To advance innovation and creativity, we encourage researchers to break down traditional silos and foster multidisciplinary collaboration. Collaborating with experts from diverse fields such as materials science, quantum physics, computer science, and data analysis will open new perspectives and accelerate breakthroughs.

2. *Embrace Open Data and Open Source*:

To accelerate progress and maximize the collective knowledge, we advocate for the open sharing of data and research findings. Embracing open data and open-source practices enables researchers to build upon each other's work, fostering an environment of collaboration, transparency, and collective growth.

3. *Explore Unconventional Ideas:*

In the pursuit of groundbreaking discoveries, do not shy away from exploring unconventional ideas and paths less traveled. Encourage curiosity-driven research that may lead to unexpected breakthroughs. Embrace failure as an essential part of the creative process, for it often serves as a stepping stone to success.

4. *Harness the Power of AI-Driven Simulations*:

AI-driven simulations have proven to be invaluable in understanding complex systems and predicting material properties. Embrace the potential of AI-optimized simulations to accelerate the discovery of novel superconductors and quantum materials.

5. *Push the Boundaries of Quantum Computing*:

Quantum computing remains an area of immense potential and challenges. Advancing the field requires researchers to push the boundaries of quantum hardware, develop innovative quantum algorithms, and explore new applications where quantum computing can bring a significant advantage.

6. *Address Ethical and Environmental Considerations*:

As AI and superconductivity become more pervasive, it is crucial to address ethical concerns related to AI ethics, data privacy, and algorithmic biases. Additionally, consider the environmental impact of superconducting materials production and ensure sustainable practices in research and implementation.

7. *Collaborate with Industry and Government*:

To translate research into real-world applications, foster strong partnerships with industry and government agencies. Collaborations can facilitate the adoption of innovative technologies, bring research to market, and address pressing societal challenges.

8. *Nurture the Next Generation*:

Inspire and nurture the next generation of scientists, engineers, and visionaries to join the field. Encourage diversity and inclusion, creating an environment that embraces fresh perspectives and novel ideas.

Conclusion:

The fusion of AI and superconductivity holds immense promise for transforming our world, ushering in a future where humanity's potential knows no bounds. By embracing innovation, collaboration, and interdisciplinary approaches, researchers can break more ground and unlock the true potential of this dynamic partnership. Let us embark on this journey with a sense of awe and optimism, working together to shape a brighter, sustainable future where the unimaginable becomes reality. As we continue to seek solutions and open the eye of knowledge wider than ever before, let the fusion of AI and superconductivity be the catalyst that propels us towards a world of boundless possibilities and unparalleled discoveries. Together, we hold the power to shape a future limited only by our collective imagination.